Kryptonite for Bullies

Kryptonite for Bullies

Written and Illustrated
by
C.Butenhoff

ISBN 978-1-09838-494-4

First Edition

Written and Illustrated by Charles Butenhoff

Published by BookBaby Publishing. 7905 N. Crescent Blvd. Pennsauken, NJ 08110

Contact information: artcproducts@gmail.com

This book is printed in U.S.A.

With fond memories
and esteem to

Ralph Waldo Emerson
Theodor Seuss Geisel
Shel Silverstein
and
Stan Lee

Introduction

This book is about my life. Well, 90% of it anyway. Nearly all my life I've dealt with bullies in one way or another. As a young boy, growing up in a family of seven, we routinely changed homes (lost count after 25 moves). Those home disruptions led to dealing with the physical and mental stress of moving, as well as the cultural stigma and cruelty of those who believed they were better than you, judging your family's economical status, how you look, and your place in the bullying heirarchy. Unfortunately this was pervasive in my young life, as it is in many of our young people's lives. I tried to fit in by participating in sports and in the classroom (art, choir & phy. ed. were my favorites, and with those staff where I felt their safety and trust). Those involvements helped, especially in meeting a greater section of my 9th grade class, but it didn't stop the bullying for me or many of my classmates. Thankfully, toward the end of my freshman year in High School, we had an ephiphany. Fed up with the harassment, and gaining trust In some school staff, we decided that the physical pain which may incur by standing up to the bullies couldn't possibly be any worse than the physical and emotional pain we were already experiencing on nearly a weekly basis. We decided to put our risky notion into action.

As our new strategy evolved, our fear began to diminish within our group of friends knowing we had each other's backs. We realized that our new appearance had the bullies withdrawing in their quest to intimidate. Most of my classmates bought into the philosophy in caring for each other, no matter our clique. We banded together in watching over those who were being harassed. It truly changed the culture of our class, especially compared to the other classes above us in age. We continued this caring and protecting approach with each other throughout the remainder of our high school years, and we honestly felt comfortable with each other. It was wonderful. Upon entering college, I would have never predicted an Education degree with teaching and coaching at middle and high school levels. My degrees in Art and Special Education allowed me to watch and learn from a wide variety of students. As I learned from my students, and then added in my own high school experiences, a creation and implementation of a bullying deterant philosophy took hold. I shared this philosophy with students who had similar concerns in their daily lives. Those conversations only needed my retirement of teaching for the illustrated version to be realized. That extra time is now represented in "Kryptonite for Bullies". My hope is that this book can be a framework if you're troubled by similar experiences. God bless you in your quest to be a valued member, model, and mentor to those you care about and in wanting them to have a more successful and joyful existence.

Kryptonite

for

Bullies

We've all felt it as girls, boys,
women and men.
When you think the bullies are gone,
only to feel their cruelty again.
But the knights of old
and the heroes of today,
know the keys to fight bullies
and send them away.

How do they do it? Would you like to know?
How to rid us of bullies and the hurt they sow?
If you turn these pages, you too will learn,
how knights and heroes act and what they earn.

In fighting bullies, this first trait is a must.
Surround yourself with people and family you trust.
Trust is knowing that they'll stand by you,
with their hearts and minds in believing what's true...
We should all feel safe in what we live and do.

Don't be afraid to say goodbye,
to friends who have chosen too often to lie.

It's hard to stay true from beginning to end,
but trust is the trait you must have in a friend.

In a true friend there is nothing stronger,
it's our trust which makes our hearts grow fonder.

Patience, really?, to deal with a bully?
That doesn't make sense or even seem right.
But patience is the key when it comes to a fight.
Patience doesn't mean "rollover" - "play dead."
Patience means, "stop," "think," "use your head."

The last thing we want is to become like them.
So... wait, think, and make a plan with a friend.
Power is what bullies feel and need.
It's the hole in their heart that they must feed.
Being smart takes time and patience to apply it.
Thought wins over power. Remember David and Goliath?

So, please, please, be patient my friend.
Good over evil will prevail in the end.
Just take a deep breath and keep your cool.
Bullies wimper away when they feel like a fool.

Patience takes courage when you're afraid.
And courage is still lacking in the world these days.
It's always been this way, "the strong and the meek".
We were meant to right wrongs and to protect the weak

To look that bully in the eyes,
and then watch them slowly realize,
they have no power over us,
no matter how they tweet, talk, hit, or cuss.
Courage comes with true friends and trust.
Bullies are liars and not like us.
We're like a Bullies Kryptonite.
Our courage with friends in doing what's right.
It saps a bully's power and destroys their might.
Courage lets bullies know that we will fight.
That we're not afraid, and won't run in fright.

You see, bullies aren't really all that tough.
They only know how to lie, cheat, and be rough.
Courage in our actions, in what we do and say,
will band good people together and scare bullies away.

Ask yourself,
"what's important to you?"
Do you do what you say and then follow through?
That's Integrity when you say and do it.
You promise something and then follow through it.
Integrity is what we want in all of our friends.
Through the ups and downs, the curves and the bends.
A person with integrity has grit in life.
You can count on them, no matter the strife.
They will deliver their trust and courage for you.
They will honor this trait for the sake of truth.

If you have integrity, you are truly a treasure.
It's the most sought after virtue by any measure.
We ask it of others, in hopes that they're true.
It should be the same for us,
not just what we say, but what we do.

When we judge people, and you can add bullies to that list,
we may sound too perfect and put our humility at risk.
Being humble is as important as any other trait.
Acting better than someone is not how we rate.
Humility is knowing that we all make mistakes.
We learn from them,
we grow from them,
in our quest to be great.
Greatness comes from believing you're not.
Using these traits to help others, without being a "big shot".
There's nothing greater than one who's more skilled than others,
but humbly shows respect for another.

The last virtue to learn, may be asking a lot.
Cuz not everyone's thankful for what they've got.
It could be me, or you, or them,
when it seems sad things happen again and again.
Like all the virtues, believing isn't easy sometimes.
But try to be grateful for something.
Start with sunshine!

Be grateful for things we take for granted.
How about friends, or pets, or gardens planted!
Gratitude helps us to believe,
that no matter the problem, there's good to achieve.
Like knowing these virtues of our knights and heroes,
and helping those feeling like losers and zeros.

We all have these virtues in our heart.
Make a vow to yourself that you're willing to start
by living these traits and doing your part.

Now, go gather people you love and trust. Remember, strength in numbers is a must.

Share with them these skills you've read and the eras of knights and heroes aren't dead. Make a decision to go and do what's right. Carry on the quest of a "Bully's Kryptonite".

C. Butenhoff was raised in Montana and Minnesota where he grew up loving art, hunting, fishing, sports, cowboying, and the friendships that made them all fantastic life molding experiences. After more than 30 years in public education as an Art and Special Education Instructor, his retirement has allowed him more time to enjoy his home in the country, creating drawings, paintings, sculpture, pottery, and hopefully more books. He currently resides in rural Minnesota on a small farm, encouraged by his wife, children, grandchildren, family, friends, and animals-wild and domestic.

Email contacts can be made artCproducts@gmail.com
Artwork and contacts at charlesbutenhoff.com

Acknowledgments

Many people are responsible for the possibility of this book being published. First of all, thanks to you for reading my book. I hope that you found some acknowledgement of your own, or for someone you know who has gone through bullying. People in Education see far too much sadness, stress, and self-harm in our students and their families. Unfortunately, these realities are not new and not diminishing. I thank the teachers, cooks, custodians, secretaries, and aides in my elementary and secondary schools who encouraged me when I appeared down and defeated. Those caring actions and words are the molding moments in a young person's life that get us all through any heartbreaking difficult times. I also want to thank all of my co-workers throughout my career as a Public School Educator. Without them I wouldn't have known if I was doing it right or missing the mark competely. My students were my best instructors. They constantly kept me aware of what was truly important each day. Somedays it was the lesson, somedays it was the current event, but it was, and always should be, a shared valid moment in a relationship that may make or break that person's day, week, or life.

Lastly, I must thank my family for having empathy for me and my profession. My wife Therese, and my three children, Ashley, Connor, and Maren have always understood my passion about the gravity of public education, peer pressure, social media, and the real life consequences that go along with it. My family and life long friends are the people I trust in my earthly universe. Without them nothing else would be possible. Any success I may achieve falls firmly on their shoulders from their encouragement of my skills and their forgiveness of my many shortcomings.

Thank you. God's blessings.

"We will have to repent in this generation not merely for the vitriolic words and actions of the bad people, but for the appalling silence of the good people".

Martin Luther King Jr.

Kryptonite for Bullies Discussion Points

The main points of this book are to describe and instill personality traits in our young people that will help them handle future stressful interpersonal situations. These traits are not specifically just for use in bullying, but also in building successful relationships with all acquaintances.

The postitive traits in our book readings are *Trust, Patience, Courage, Integrity, Humility, and Gratitude.* The following sections are topical points that may further aide in the depth of conversations you may have with your children/students.

Trait #1: *Trust*
As in our reading, *Trust* begins with the people around us. Without *Trust* in our lives no other worthwhile interpersonal connections will succeed. That distress will extend into all other factions of our lives. That's why *Trust* is the building block of all the personal needs and traits.

Discussion Points:
*Who do you *trust* in your life right now? What have they specifically done to earn your *trust*?

*Who do you not *trust*? What have they done that has lost your *trust*? Is there anything we can do to earn *trust* back?

*Establish the *trustworthy* people in each of our daily settings or environments. Develop a step by step plan that will ensure our ability to seek and secure those special people for help if and when we need it.

Trait #2: *Patience*
Patience is knowing how to wait with our words and actions during a stressful situation.

Discussion Points:
*Do you notice when you are the most *impatient*? What is it that bugs you the most?

*Is there someone you admire as a *patient* person? How do you think they are able to remain *patient*?

*Discuss standard techniques that people can learn to build personal *patience*. Such as these, or others:
    -understand your own reasons for the things that bug you, it's called "self-reflection".
    -slow down. take a breath. stop. think.
    -learn to meditate and and become mindful.
    -practice what you're going to do in those known upcoming stressful times
    -practice restraint in the small things of your life. Like choosing not do your everyday habits to excess, or denying yourself the little things you really don't need.

*Discuss how the traits of *patience* are a true reflection of personal confidence and strength. That confidence is felt from within and observed outwardly by others. Everyone wants to have a person around them who is "cool in a heated situation".

Trait #3: *Courage*

In our reading, *Courage* was visualized in the person of Rosa Parks. It's certainly worthwhile to discuss the history of the incredible *courage* it took Rosa on that bus. But it's also important to discuss daily examples of people who stand up for what's morally right, even knowing that the consequences of their *courage* may end up to be personally painful or stressful.

Discussion Points:

*In the example of Rosa Parks, discuss historical acts of *courage* (check out the back cover of this book).

*Discuss everday people we know whom we consider to be *courageous*, why we think so, and honor their story.

*Does the possibility of pain, whether physical or emotional, keep us from being *courageous*? Discuss how we all feel that struggle, that it's part of our being, and it doesn't make us bad or weak.

*Discuss what our "redline" is when we will accept the risk of personal pain in proceeding with an act of moral *courage.*

*Do we have to risk our life or save someone else's to be *courageous*? Discuss everyday *courageous things* we can all do for ourselves and others.

Trait #4: *Integrity*

Integrity is stating what we believe and then following through and doing it. It's the trait we expect and demand from everyone around us, yet it disappoints us the most.

Discussion Points:
*Discuss what "Walk the Talk" means to us.

*Who are examples of people we think show *integrity*?

*What are some daily challenges that test our *integrity*?

*We will all lose our *integrity* at one time or another. We will make a promise we won't keep. When that happens, what can we do to regain our *integrity*? How can we ensure ourselves this particular event will be just a one time thing?

Trait #5: *Humility*
Successfully living *humility* is a difficult paradox. We want to feel and show confidence in being the best at what we do, but... we don't want people to believe that **we** think we're the best in what we say and do. As in the line from our book, "greatness comes from believing you're not". We must teach and believe that confidence comes from our diligence in the repetition of our practice and hard work. *Humility* comes from knowing that our hard work and confidence are to be shown in actions, not words. People who are the best at what they do know there's always the next level to achieve and that perfection is a journey, not necessarily a final destination. *Humility* is not weakness, it's empathy for others and confidence in yourself.

Discussion Points:
*Discuss well known successful people across a variety of disciplines and how we believe they achieved such status. Does their skillful success also exhibit *humility*?

*Contrast the difference in the "likability" of people who have great skill and of the people who have great skill and *humility*?

*Compare examples of arrogance versus confidence.

*Who are people in our daily lives that show us *humility* and confidence? How can we emulate their techniques?

Trait #6: *Gratitude*

Gratitude is a difficult trait to believe in if you constantly live in distress. How can I be *thankful* about being teased, harassed, or abused? How can I be *gracious* about living in poverty? How can I have *gratitude* when my family members are hurting or sick? Learning *gratitude* has to be understood like all the other traits. But unlike the other traits, discussing *gratitude* takes much more conscientious empathy and tactful delivery in its instruction for each person's individual situation.

Discussion Points:

*Discuss the concept that everyone has their own sadness and no one person's is more important than another. Relate each person's experiences with the concept of "empathy".

*Explore how empathy for others will help us develop our own *gratefulness* for what we have in our lives.

*Discuss specific things in each person's life that make them happy (music, sports, games, people, animals, etc.) Examine how we can integrate those enjoyments into our daily lives, building a life long strategy to happiness and success. Our passions, even at a young age, are our strengths, which may also help us determine our vocation.

*Revisiting the 6 positive traits from our book, *(Trust, Patience, Courage, Integrity, Humility, Gratitude)*, point out and praise any of those traits that you already recognize in your child. Emphasize that just like our Super Heroes and Knights, we all have our strengths and weaknesses. There will always be villians or trials in our lives. That's why it needs to be an ongoing quest to find and keep trustworthy people in our day, showing ourselves that we have the skills to be happy, caring, and successful.

"A hero is no braver than an ordinary man, but he is brave five minutes longer",

Ralph Waldo Emerson

Dr. Charles A. Eastman
Sacagewea
Cesar Chavez
Sonia Sotomayer
Dolores Huerta
Martin Luther King Jr.
Minoru Yasui
Neil Armstrong
Ruth Bader Ginsburg
Laronda Marshall
Darby Voeks
Glen Bihler

Chief Joseph
Abraham Lincoln
Harriet Tubman
Susan B. Anthony
Rosa Parks
Yuji Ichioka
Audie Murphy
Jonas Salk
Derrick Bryd
Chris Vinton
Dick Hoyt
Grant Synder

Darius Dillard and Nate Williams

These are just some of our wonderful American Heroes.

Could we add your name to the list?...

"Heroes and knights are no braver than an ordinary person, but they are brave five minutes longer".

ISBN 978-1-09838-494-4

CREATIVE WRITING PROMPTS

AGES
8–12

FOR KIDS

ELEANOR THOMPSON